Managing Through Change:
Leaders

© Matthew Miles, 2024
All rights reserved.

No part of this publication may be reproduced, distributed, or transmitted in any form or by any means, including photocopying, recording, or other electronic or mechanical methods, without the prior written permission of the author, except in the case of brief quotations embodied in critical reviews and certain other non-commercial uses permitted by copyright law.

This book is a work of non-fiction. Every effort has been made to ensure the accuracy of the information presented within, but the author and publisher accept no responsibility for any errors or omissions. The content is provided for informational purposes only and is not intended as a substitute for professional advice or guidance.

Published by Matthew Miles

Disclaimer: The opinions expressed in this book are those of the author and do not reflect the views of NHS England or any other affiliated organisations.

For permissions or enquiries, contact:
contact@fullick-miles.net

To Steve, Jerome, Denzel, and Mya—
Your love, support, and encouragement mean everything to me. This book would not have been possible without each of you. Thank you for being my anchor, my inspiration, and my biggest cheerleaders. This is for all of us.

Table of contents

Introduction *1*

Understanding Change in the NHS Context *4*

Types of Change 4
    Structural Change 4
    Cultural Change 6
    Technological Change 7

Unique Challenges 9
    Public Accountability and Patient-Centric Care 9

Resistance in a Unionised Environment 10

The Human Side of Change 11
    The Kubler-Ross Change Curve 12

What the NHS Can Learn from Other Organisations 13

Bringing It All Together 14

The Psychology of Change *15*

Understanding How People Respond to Change: Bridges' Transition Model 15
    1. Ending, Losing, Letting Go 15
    2. The Neutral Zone 17
    3. The New Beginning 18

Recognising Change Fatigue 19

Common Symptoms of Change Fatigue 19

Building Psychological Safety 21

Why Psychological Safety Matters During Change....................21

Practical Techniques for Building Psychological Safety 21

Using Tools to Foster Psychological Safety 22

Bringing It All Together 23

The NHS Manager's Role in Change 24

The Importance of Transparent Communication..............24

Why Transparency Matters 24

Strategies for Transparent Communication..................................25

Balancing Empathy with Authority 26

The Role of Empathy 26

The Role of Authority 27

Strategies for Balancing Empathy and Authority 27

Staying Aligned with Organisational Values While Advocating for Your Team 28

Why Organisational Values Matter..28

Advocating for Your Team 29

Strategies for Balancing Values and Advocacy 30

Bringing It All Together 30

Practical Strategies for Managing Change 31

Developing a Change Plan..31

Setting clear goals and milestones. 31

Identifying quick wins to build momentum 33

iv

Communicating Effectively During Change 34
Using the Right Channels 34
Ensuring Messages Are Clear, Consistent, and Timely 35

Involving Your Team 36
Gathering Feedback to Increase Buy-In 36
Recognising and Addressing Concerns Early 37

Supporting Individuals 38
Using Dynamic Conversations to Check in on Well-Being 38
Recognising and Mitigating Signs of Burnout 39

Bringing It All Together 40

Addressing Resistance and Building Resilience *42*

Understanding Resistance 42
Why People Resist Change 42
Techniques to Address Resistance Empathetically 44

Fostering Resilience 45
Encouraging a Growth Mindset 46
Celebrating Small Successes and Maintaining Morale 47
Maintaining Morale During Change 48

Bringing It All Together 49

Case Studies and Lessons Learned *51*

Example 1: Managing a team through the NHS England merger 51
Situation 51
Task 52

Actions Taken 52
Results 54

Example 2: Implementing digital systems in a Trust 55

Situation 55
Task 55
Actions Taken 56
Results 57

Reflections on Case Studies 58

Key Takeaways 58

Tools and Templates *60*

Template: Change Communication Plan 60

1. Objectives 60
2. Stakeholder Analysis 60
3. Communication Channels 61
4. Timeline 61
5. Feedback Mechanisms 62

Checklist: Key Steps for Managing Change in the NHS .. 62

Tool: Resilience-Building Activities for Teams 64

Activity 1: Growth Mindset Reflections 64
Activity 2: Celebrating Small Wins 65
Activity 3: Resilience Mapping 65

Bringing It All Together 66

Reflection and Next Steps *67*

Encouraging Reflection 67

Questions for Reflection...67

Actionable Steps to Implement Lessons 68

1. Develop a Change Plan 68
2. Enhance Communication Practices 69
3. Foster Team Involvement..69
4. Build Psychological Safety 70
5. Celebrate Successes..70

Where to Go for Additional Support 70

NHS Resources 71
External Training Opportunities..71
Chartered Management Institute (CMI) 71
Peer Networks and Communities..72

Final Thoughts.. 72

Conclusion 74

The Importance of Proactive, Compassionate Leadership..........74
Empowering Managers to Lead Confidently 75
Looking Ahead...76

About the author 78

Call to action 81

Introduction

Change is an inevitable part of life, but in the NHS, it often feels like the only constant. Whether it's a merger, restructuring, the implementation of new technologies, or responding to external pressures, NHS managers are tasked with leading teams through challenges that can seem relentless. If you've picked up this book, it's likely because you're in the midst of navigating change—or you're preparing for it—and are searching for practical advice to guide your team while staying grounded yourself.

This book was born out of my own experiences as a leader in the NHS. Over the years, I've had the privilege—and sometimes the challenge—of leading teams through significant organisational transitions. I've seen what works, what doesn't, and what has unexpected consequences. I've witnessed the toll that uncertainty takes on morale, how it erodes trust, and how it can lead to disengagement if left unchecked. But I've also seen the power of clear communication, empathy, and resilience to transform even the most difficult situations into opportunities for growth. I've learned that good leadership isn't about having all the answers; it's about creating an environment where teams feel supported, valued, and empowered to adapt to whatever comes next.

The NHS is unlike any other organisation. Our work is deeply intertwined with the lives and health of millions of people. We aren't just managing processes or budgets; we're leading teams who directly or indirectly impact patient outcomes every day. This dual responsibility—to both our teams and the people they serve—makes managing change within the NHS uniquely rewarding but also uniquely complex. The stakes are high, and the pressure to deliver can feel unrelenting. Yet, the impact of good leadership in these moments can't be overstated. It has the potential to not only carry a team through turbulent times but to emerge stronger, more cohesive, and more effective.

In this guide, I aim to share what I've learned about managing change in the NHS. This isn't a theoretical textbook, nor is it filled with jargon or generic advice. Instead, it's a practical resource grounded in real-world experience. We'll explore the psychology of change—how individuals and teams react to it and what you can do to help them through it. We'll discuss strategies for effective communication, building resilience, and addressing resistance. Along the way, I'll provide practical tools and templates you can use to plan, communicate, and implement change in a way that works for your unique circumstances.

One of the greatest challenges of leading through change is balancing empathy with action. As leaders, we need to recognise the very human responses to uncertainty—fear, anxiety, and resistance—while also moving forward with confidence and clarity. It's a fine line to walk, but with the right tools and mindset, it's one you can navigate successfully. This guide will help you strike that balance, equipping you to lead your team with compassion and confidence.

Change, by its very nature, is hard. It disrupts routines, creates uncertainty, and forces people out of their comfort zones. Yet, it's also an opportunity for innovation, growth, and progress. The way we respond to change—both as individuals and as leaders—determines whether it becomes a stumbling block or a stepping stone. My hope is that this book provides you with the clarity, strategies, and reassurance you need to turn the challenges of change into opportunities for success.

Whether you're a seasoned manager or stepping into leadership for the first time, this guide is for you. It's for those who want to lead not just effectively but empathetically. It's for those who believe that good leadership is about more than hitting targets—it's about building trust, fostering collaboration, and helping people thrive even in the face of uncertainty.

Let's get started. Together, we'll explore the tools, techniques, and mindsets that can help you lead your team confidently through change and make a lasting impact on your organisation. Change isn't easy, but with the right approach, it can be transformative.

- Matt

Understanding Change in the NHS Context

Change in the NHS is not just frequent; it is a defining characteristic of the organisation. Whether structural, cultural, or technological, these changes ripple across every layer, impacting teams, patients, and systems. For NHS managers, navigating change effectively requires a combination of strategic insight, practical skills, and an empathetic approach to leadership.

In this chapter, we'll delve into the three key types of change—structural, cultural, and technological—explore the unique challenges NHS managers face, and offer practical strategies for navigating transitions. Along the way, we'll reflect on how these approaches align with NHS values of compassion, inclusion, and collaboration.

Types of Change

NHS managers encounter three primary types of change: structural, cultural, and technological. While each presents unique challenges, they often intersect, requiring managers to adopt a multi-faceted approach.

Structural Change

Structural changes are among the most visible and often the most disruptive. These involve reorganising departments, merging organisations, or creating new systems of accountability. Examples include major mergers such as the integration of NHS England, NHS Digital, and Health Education England, or the establishment of Integrated Care Systems (ICSs). These changes aim to streamline processes and improve outcomes but can create uncertainty and anxiety among staff.

Example

During the 2022 NHS England merger, many staff found themselves unsure about their roles and reporting lines. A lack of clarity created widespread anxiety, and trust in leadership was strained. In one of my roles, I saw this uncertainty manifest in disengagement and resistance. To address these challenges, I introduced weekly team check-ins where staff could share concerns, ask questions, and receive updates. While these sessions didn't resolve every issue, they provided a vital space for transparency and trust-building. Staff felt heard, even if definitive answers weren't always available.

Key Takeaways for Managers

Communicate early and consistently: Share updates as soon as possible, even if the details aren't finalised. Being transparent builds trust.

Involve staff in solutions: Ask for input on how new structures could work better. This fosters a sense of ownership and reduces resistance.

Acknowledge uncertainty: Avoid the temptation to "over-reassure." Instead, acknowledge what you don't yet know and set expectations for when updates will come.

> **Reflective Questions**
> *How does your team typically respond to structural changes? Are there opportunities to involve them earlier in shaping the transition?*

Cultural Change

Cultural change focuses on shifting values, behaviours, and norms within an organisation. In the NHS, cultural initiatives such as the **NHS People Promise** or the focus on psychological safety require managers to inspire staff to embrace new ways of working. Cultural change can be subtle and long-term, making it particularly challenging to embed effectively.

Example

In one of my teams, implementing the People Promise values met with initial scepticism. Staff felt the principles of inclusion and collaboration were "corporate speak" that didn't resonate with their day-to-day experiences. I realised that embedding these values required visible and consistent action. I began by modelling the behaviours I wanted to see, such as actively seeking diverse perspectives in meetings and recognising inclusive practices publicly. Over time, these actions helped shift perceptions, and the team began to see the values as meaningful rather than rhetorical.

Key Takeaways for Managers

Lead by example: Behaviours are contagious. Demonstrate the values you want to instil in your team.

Encourage open dialogue: Create safe spaces for staff to discuss their concerns and share their interpretations of cultural change.

Celebrate progress: Recognise and reward staff when they embody the desired cultural shifts.

> **Reflective Questions**
>
> *What small actions can you take today to model the behaviours you want your team to adopt?*
> *Are there ways to highlight "quick wins" that reinforce cultural change?*

Technological Change

Technological change has become a cornerstone of NHS transformation, with digital tools and systems promising to improve efficiency, reduce errors, and enhance patient care. However, these changes often come with challenges, including resistance from staff, steep learning curves, and integration difficulties.

Example

In a previous role, I led the implementation of a digital radiology referral system to replace a paper-based process. Initially, staff were resistant. Some feared the technology would make their roles redundant, while others doubted their ability to adapt. By involving the team in pilot testing, providing tailored training, and ensuring ongoing support, we shifted perceptions over time. Staff became advocates for the system, which ultimately improved patient outcomes and reduced administrative burdens.

Key Takeaways for Managers

Start small: Piloting new technology in a single department allows you to refine processes and build success stories before a wider rollout.

Empower champions: Identify enthusiastic staff members to act as advocates and trainers for their peers.

Tailor training: Ensure training sessions address specific concerns and skill gaps within your team.

> **Reflective Questions**
>
> *Have you involved your team in the design or testing phases of new technology?*
>
> *How can you make training more relevant and engaging for your staff?*

Unique Challenges

Managing change in the NHS comes with unique challenges that set it apart from other organisations. These include balancing public accountability with patient-centric care and navigating resistance within a heavily unionised environment.

Public Accountability and Patient-Centric Care

The NHS operates under intense scrutiny from the government, media, and public. Changes must balance efficiency with the delivery of high-quality patient care, which adds complexity to decision-making.

Example

The rollout of Integrated Care Systems (ICSs) aimed to improve collaboration between health and social care providers, ultimately benefiting patients. However, the speed of implementation left many teams scrambling to adjust while maintaining continuity of care. In my experience, framing changes in terms of patient outcomes helped staff understand the broader purpose, even when the immediate process felt disruptive.

Key Takeaways for Managers

Communicate patient benefits: Help staff see how changes align with the NHS's mission to improve patient outcomes.

Provide regular updates: Transparency fosters trust, even during challenging transitions.

Reflective Questions

Are you clearly articulating how changes will benefit patients? How can you involve staff in discussions about patient-centred outcomes?

Resistance in a Unionised Environment

The NHS is one of the most heavily unionised workforces in the UK, which can create challenges during change initiatives. While unions play a vital role in protecting staff, they can also amplify resistance if concerns aren't addressed early.

Example

During the rollout of an e-rostering system, union representatives raised concerns about fairness and work-life balance. By engaging them early, listening to their input, and adapting the implementation to address their feedback, we avoided significant conflict. The resulting system met organisational goals while addressing staff concerns.

Key Takeaways for Managers

Engage unions early: Treat union representatives as partners in the change process rather than obstacles.

Address concerns directly: Proactively seek input from unions to identify and mitigate potential issues.

> **Reflective Questions**
> *How can you build stronger relationships with union representatives in your organisation?*
> *Are there mechanisms in place to address staff concerns early in the process?*

The Human Side of Change

Change is not just an operational challenge; it is an emotional one. It disrupts routines, creates uncertainty, and often triggers resistance. Understanding these responses and addressing them with empathy is critical to successful leadership.

The Kubler-Ross Change Curve

The **Kubler-Ross Change Curve** offers a framework for understanding how individuals respond to change. It includes four key stages:

1. **Denial:** "This won't affect me."
2. **Resistance:** "This will make things worse."
3. **Exploration:** "How can I adapt to this?"
4. **Commitment:** "This is starting to work."

In one instance, introducing a new rota system sparked immediate resistance among staff, who felt it was unfair and burdensome. Acknowledging their frustrations, involving them in refining the system, and celebrating small improvements helped shift their perspective from resistance to acceptance.

Practical Techniques for Managers

Listen actively: Pay attention to verbal and non-verbal cues during team meetings to identify resistance.

Use anonymous surveys: Gauge morale and identify concerns without putting staff on the spot.

Acknowledge emotions: Validate staff frustrations and fears to create a foundation for dialogue.

> **Reflective Questions**
> *How does your team typically express resistance?*
> *Are there ways to create safer spaces for staff to share their concerns?*

What the NHS Can Learn from Other Organisations

While the NHS is unique, there are lessons to be learned from other sectors about managing change effectively.

Procter & Gamble (P&G): Known for its structured approach to change, P&G uses the **ADKAR model** (Awareness, Desire, Knowledge, Ability, Reinforcement) to guide transitions. This method could easily be adapted to NHS settings, particularly in training and communication strategies.

Airbnb: During a major restructuring, Airbnb's CEO held open forums where employees could ask questions and express concerns. This transparency helped maintain trust during a challenging period, a principle NHS managers can apply by creating open communication channels.

Key Takeaways
- Borrow structured models like ADKAR to guide staff through change.
- Prioritise transparency to maintain trust during uncertainty.

Bringing It All Together

Change in the NHS is inevitable but manageable. By understanding the types of change, anticipating challenges, and addressing the human side of transitions, NHS managers can lead with confidence, empathy, and clarity. Success lies in aligning your strategies with NHS values of compassion, inclusion, and collaboration, ensuring that both staff and patients benefit from the transformation.

As we move forward, the next section will delve deeper into the psychology of change, offering further tools and strategies to support teams during periods of uncertainty. Together, we'll build a roadmap for navigating change effectively and sustainably.

The Psychology of Change

Change is not just an operational or logistical challenge; it's a deeply personal experience that triggers a range of emotional responses. For NHS managers, understanding how individuals and teams react to change is critical to leading effectively. Whether introducing new policies, merging teams, or implementing technology, the human element of change often determines the success or failure of the initiative.

This section explores the psychology of change through **Bridges' Transition Model**, examines the common symptoms of change fatigue, and highlights the importance of building psychological safety to support staff through uncertainty.

Understanding How People Respond to Change: Bridges' Transition Model

One of the most insightful frameworks for understanding the human response to change is **William Bridges' Transition Model**. Bridges emphasises that change is external—it's what happens around us—but transition is internal. Transition is the psychological process people go through to adapt to change, and it occurs in three stages:

1. Ending, Losing, Letting Go

This stage marks the initial reaction to change and is often accompanied by a sense of loss. People must let go of the old ways of working, familiar routines, or even relationships. Resistance is common here because individuals may feel anxious, uncertain, or even angry about what they are losing.

Example

When a new e-rostering system was introduced in one of my teams, the immediate reaction from staff was frustration and scepticism. They feared the new system would complicate their workflows and disrupt their well-established routines. Some vocalised their resistance openly, while others disengaged silently.

How Managers Can Support

Acknowledge the Loss: Recognise and validate feelings of loss. For example, in team meetings, acknowledge how the change impacts current practices and invite staff to share their concerns.

Provide Clarity: Clearly explain why the change is necessary and what benefits it will bring.

Offer Support: Provide resources, such as training or one-on-one sessions, to help staff adapt.

> **Reflective Question**
>
> *How often do you acknowledge the emotional toll of change in your team? Are there ways you can address concerns more proactively?*

2. The Neutral Zone

This stage is a transitional period where the old ways are gone, but the new ones haven't fully taken hold. It's often a time of confusion, low morale, and uncertainty. While this stage can feel uncomfortable, it's also a time of creativity and growth as people begin to explore new possibilities.

Example

During the rollout of Integrated Care Systems (ICSs), many teams found themselves in this "in-between" stage. Old organisational boundaries were removed, but new relationships and workflows were still being developed. In my experience, this ambiguity left some staff feeling directionless, while others began to experiment with new collaborative approaches.

How Managers Can Support

Encourage Experimentation: Allow staff to test new ideas and approaches without fear of failure.

Maintain Regular Communication: Share updates frequently to reduce uncertainty, even if there's little new information to report.

Promote Team Bonding: Use this time to strengthen relationships within teams by organising team-building activities or informal check-ins.

Reflective Question

How does your team cope with ambiguity? Are you creating opportunities for them to experiment and adapt?

---

3. The New Beginning

In this final stage, people begin to embrace the change. They understand their roles within the new system, and energy levels start to rise as they see the benefits of the change. However, reaching this stage requires careful nurturing.

Example

In a project to digitise manual radiology referrals, the turning point came when staff saw measurable improvements in patient outcomes and time savings. This tangible evidence helped them fully commit to the new system.

How Managers Can Support

Celebrate Milestones: Recognise and reward progress, both big and small. For example, highlight team achievements in meetings or emails.

Provide Reinforcement: Offer continuous training and feedback to ensure the new ways of working become second nature.

Reinforce Purpose: Remind staff of how their efforts contribute to the organisation's goals and patient outcomes.

> **Reflective Question**
>
> *Are you recognising and celebrating your team's progress? How can you reinforce their sense of purpose during transitions?*

Recognising Change Fatigue

In organisations like the NHS, where change is constant, **change fatigue** is a common issue. Change fatigue occurs when staff feel overwhelmed by the volume or pace of changes, leading to disengagement, burnout, or resistance.

Common Symptoms of Change Fatigue

- **Decreased Morale:** Teams may exhibit low energy or enthusiasm for new initiatives.

- **Increased Absenteeism:** Staff may take more sick days due to stress or burnout.
- **Resistance to New Initiatives:** Employees may push back against even minor changes, citing "initiative overload."
- **Declining Performance:** Productivity and quality of work may drop as staff struggle to keep up with new demands.

Example

In one of my roles, the rapid rollout of multiple digital systems in quick succession left staff feeling exhausted. Although each system promised efficiency, the cumulative effect of learning new workflows, attending training sessions, and adapting to change created widespread frustration. Some team members openly resisted further changes, while others became disengaged.

How Managers Can Mitigate Change Fatigue

1. **Prioritise Changes:** Not every change needs to happen simultaneously. Work with leadership to prioritise initiatives and stagger their implementation.
2. **Provide Adequate Support:** Ensure that staff have the time, resources, and training needed to adapt to changes.
3. **Listen to Feedback:** Use anonymous surveys or team meetings to gauge how staff are coping and adjust your approach accordingly.
4. **Celebrate Small Wins:** Recognising progress, even incremental, can help re-energise teams.

> **Reflective Question**
>
> *Are your team members showing signs of change fatigue? How can you adjust the pace of change to better support them?*

Building Psychological Safety

One of the most effective ways to help teams navigate change is by creating an environment of **psychological safety**. Coined by Amy Edmondson, psychological safety refers to a climate where individuals feel safe to express their thoughts, ask questions, and admit mistakes without fear of judgment or retribution.

Why Psychological Safety Matters During Change

Encourages Honest Feedback: Staff are more likely to share concerns or ideas if they feel their voices will be heard.

Reduces Resistance: When people feel safe, they're more open to experimenting with new approaches.

Supports Wellbeing: Psychological safety fosters trust and reduces the anxiety often associated with change.

Practical Techniques for Building Psychological Safety

1. **Model Vulnerability:** Share your own experiences with change, including challenges and lessons learned. For

example, during a team meeting, you might say, "I struggled with this process too when I first encountered it. Here's how I approached it."

2. **Encourage Open Dialogue:** Create regular opportunities for staff to voice their concerns or ask questions, such as team check-ins or one-to-one meetings.
3. **Respond Constructively to Mistakes:** When mistakes happen, treat them as learning opportunities rather than failures.
4. **Recognise Contributions:** Publicly acknowledge and celebrate team members who take risks or try new approaches.

Example

During the rollout of a new data entry system, I noticed that junior staff hesitated to admit they didn't fully understand the new process. To address this, I shared a story about a mistake I'd made while learning a similar system and how I resolved it. This openness encouraged others to speak up and seek help without fear of judgment.

Using Tools to Foster Psychological Safety

Anonymous Surveys: Use tools like Microsoft Forms to collect honest feedback without putting individuals on the spot.

Dynamic Conversations: Leverage NHS-specific frameworks for one-to-one discussions that address health, well-being, and performance.

Team Agreements: Collaboratively establish ground rules for how the team will handle feedback, disagreements, and experimentation.

> **Reflective Question**
> *How psychologically safe does your team feel right now? Are there steps you can take to encourage more openness and trust?*

Bringing It All Together

Understanding the psychology of change is critical to leading NHS teams effectively through transitions. By applying frameworks like Bridges' Transition Model, recognising the symptoms of change fatigue, and fostering psychological safety, managers can support their teams emotionally while driving progress. Change may be inevitable, but with empathy, open communication, and a focus on wellbeing, it can also be a source of growth and innovation.

As you consider your own leadership style, reflect on how you can better support your team through the stages of transition, mitigate the risks of fatigue, and create a safe environment where change is embraced rather than resisted. These principles not only align with

NHS values but also lay the foundation for a healthier, more resilient workforce.

The NHS Manager's Role in Change

NHS managers are uniquely positioned to bridge the gap between organisational objectives and the day-to-day realities of their teams. Leading through change requires not only clear direction but also the ability to inspire, support, and adapt to the needs of staff. This role often involves navigating a delicate balance between competing priorities, emotions, and expectations.

This section examines three critical responsibilities of NHS managers during change: transparent communication, balancing empathy with authority, and aligning with organisational values while advocating for the needs of your team.

The Importance of Transparent Communication

Transparent communication is the backbone of effective change management. When information is shared openly and clearly, it reduces uncertainty, builds trust, and helps teams align with organisational goals. Without it, rumours and confusion can undermine even the most well-planned initiatives.

Why Transparency Matters

- **Fosters Understanding:** Staff are more likely to embrace change when they understand the reasons behind it and how it will affect their roles.

- **Mitigates Resistance:** When managers communicate openly, staff are less likely to feel excluded or blindsided, reducing resistance.
- **Supports Team Alignment:** Clear messaging ensures everyone is on the same page and working towards a common goal.

Example

In one instance, a team I supported was tasked with piloting a new care pathway that significantly altered workflows and job responsibilities. The initial announcement was vague, leaving staff unsure of what to expect. Recognising this, I collaborated with leadership to deliver detailed briefings, explaining the specific steps of the pilot, the rationale for its introduction, and how feedback from the team would be used to shape the final model. By making communication a two-way process, we addressed uncertainties early, fostering greater buy-in.

Strategies for Transparent Communication

1. **Be Consistent:** Regular updates prevent misinformation and keep staff engaged.
2. **Tailor Messaging:** Adjust your communication style based on the audience, ensuring the information is relevant and accessible.

3. **Close the Loop:** Follow up on questions or concerns raised in meetings to show that feedback is valued and acted upon.

> **Reflective Questions**
> *Are you providing your team with the clarity they need to understand and engage with change? How can you improve the consistency and relevance of your communication?*

Balancing Empathy with Authority

Change often triggers emotional responses such as fear, uncertainty, and resistance. Managers must navigate these emotions with empathy while maintaining the authority needed to drive progress. Striking this balance is key to supporting staff without losing sight of organisational priorities.

The Role of Empathy

Empathy allows managers to connect with their teams, recognising their concerns and validating their experiences. It's particularly important during periods of significant upheaval, where feelings of vulnerability and uncertainty are heightened.

Example

During a reorganisation of administrative roles in a large NHS Trust, several team members expressed concerns about job security and workload redistribution. Rather than dismissing these fears, I took time to meet individually with staff, listen to their concerns, and provide reassurance where possible. In some cases, I adjusted workloads temporarily to ease the transition. This empathetic approach helped maintain morale and built trust within the team.

The Role of Authority

While empathy is crucial, managers also need to provide clear direction and enforce accountability. Change initiatives often require difficult decisions, such as reallocating resources or restructuring roles, which must be handled with firmness and clarity.

Example

When implementing a new rota system in a clinical department, some staff resisted the change, citing personal preferences for their existing schedules. While I acknowledged their concerns, I made it clear that the new system was essential for improving service delivery. By outlining the benefits for patients and demonstrating fairness in the rota's design, I ensured compliance without compromising team cohesion.

Strategies for Balancing Empathy and Authority

1. **Acknowledge Emotions:** Create space for staff to express their feelings without fear of judgment.

2. **Set Clear Boundaries:** Define non-negotiable elements of the change process while remaining flexible in areas where adjustments are possible.
3. **Lead with Fairness:** Ensure decisions are transparent and equitable, reinforcing your credibility as a leader.

> **Reflective Questions**
>
> *Are you balancing understanding and accountability effectively in your leadership? How can you adjust your approach to better support your team?*

Staying Aligned with Organisational Values While Advocating for Your Team

NHS managers operate in a complex environment where they must uphold organisational values while also serving as advocates for their teams. This dual responsibility can create tension, particularly during periods of change when staff concerns may conflict with wider organisational priorities.

Why Organisational Values Matter

The NHS is built on a foundation of values such as compassion, inclusion, and collaboration. Managers are expected to embody these principles, even when implementing challenging changes. By aligning with these values, managers can foster trust and create a sense of shared purpose.

Example

During the transition to a new electronic patient record (EPR) system, a team of administrative staff struggled with the additional training and adjustments required. While the organisation emphasised the long-term benefits for patient care, the immediate impact on workload was significant. I worked to align the organisation's focus on patient outcomes with the team's immediate needs by advocating for extended timelines for training and securing additional support. This ensured the team felt supported without compromising the project's goals.

Advocating for Your Team

Advocacy involves ensuring your team's voices are heard and their needs are considered in decision-making processes. It also requires finding creative ways to balance these needs with organisational objectives.

Example

In a clinical setting, staff were asked to implement a new discharge protocol designed to reduce hospital stays. While the protocol was beneficial for patients, frontline staff raised concerns about the lack of consultation and the increased time required for documentation. I facilitated a feedback session with leadership to ensure these concerns were addressed, resulting in modifications to the protocol that improved both staff workflows and patient care.

Strategies for Balancing Values and Advocacy

1. **Bridge the Gap:** Act as a translator between your team and senior leadership, ensuring both perspectives are understood.
2. **Model Values:** Demonstrate organisational values in your interactions, showing your team that these principles are more than rhetoric.
3. **Empower Staff:** Encourage your team to share their insights and suggestions, fostering a culture of collaboration.

> **Reflective Question**
> *How well do your actions reflect NHS values in practice? Are you effectively advocating for your team while staying aligned with organisational priorities?*

Bringing It All Together

The role of NHS managers in change is both challenging and rewarding. By focusing on transparent communication, balancing empathy with authority, and aligning with organisational values, managers can navigate transitions effectively while supporting their teams. These principles not only drive successful outcomes but also strengthen trust, resilience, and collaboration within teams.

As you reflect on your own leadership, consider how you can better communicate with your team, balance understanding with accountability, and advocate for their needs in alignment with the NHS's core values. Change may be inevitable, but with the right approach, it can also be a powerful force for growth and improvement.

Practical Strategies for Managing Change

Managing change in the NHS requires more than a theoretical understanding of processes and frameworks. It calls for actionable strategies tailored to the complexities of healthcare environments and the emotional realities of the people involved. As a manager, your role is to guide your team through uncertainty while maintaining focus on organisational objectives and NHS values. This section provides practical approaches to planning, communicating, involving your team, and supporting individuals during change.

Developing a Change Plan

A solid change plan is the foundation for any successful transition. It provides clarity, direction, and measurable objectives, ensuring that everyone involved understands the path forward.

Setting clear goals and milestones.

Change often feels overwhelming because of its scale or perceived complexity. Breaking it down into manageable stages with clear goals and milestones helps teams maintain focus and track progress.

Key Steps for Goal Setting

1. **Define the Desired Outcome:** Begin by clearly articulating what success looks like. For example, in transitioning to a new rota system, success might mean improved staff satisfaction and optimised coverage across shifts.
2. **Set SMART Goals:** Ensure goals are **specific**, **measurable**, **achievable**, **relevant**, and **time-bound**. Instead of saying, "Improve staff training," specify, "Deliver three 90-minute training sessions within six weeks."
3. **Establish Milestones:** Break the change into smaller phases with deadlines. Milestones act as checkpoints to evaluate progress and make adjustments.

Example

In a project to digitise manual workflows for outpatient scheduling, we set phased goals:
- **Phase 1:** Train administrative staff within four weeks.
- **Phase 2:** Pilot the system in two departments over six weeks.

- **Phase 3:** Expand rollout to all departments after resolving pilot feedback.

This approach prevented staff from feeling overwhelmed by the scale of the project and allowed us to celebrate small wins along the way.

> **Reflective Question**
> *Are your goals clear and actionable? Have you identified measurable milestones to keep your team motivated?*

Identifying quick wins to build momentum

Quick wins are small, easily achievable successes that demonstrate progress and build confidence. They help overcome initial scepticism and energise teams during the early stages of change.

How to Identify Quick Wins

- **Start with Low-Risk Changes:** Focus on adjustments that require minimal effort but yield visible benefits.
- **Celebrate Early Successes:** Recognise and reward achievements publicly to boost morale.
- **Communicate Impact:** Ensure staff understand how even small victories contribute to the overall change process.

Example

When implementing a new electronic health record system, one quick win involved streamlining appointment reminders for patients. This simple feature reduced administrative workload almost immediately and highlighted the benefits of the broader system before its full rollout.

> **Reflective Question**
> *What quick wins can you identify in your current change initiative? How can you use these to build momentum?*

Communicating Effectively During Change

Communication is the lifeblood of change management. The way you deliver information can shape how your team perceives, understands, and engages with change. Effective communication is timely, clear, consistent, and delivered through appropriate channels.

Using the Right Channels

Different types of messages require different communication methods. Selecting the right channel for your message ensures it reaches the right audience with the appropriate level of formality.

Examples of Communication Channels
- **Microsoft Teams:** Ideal for informal updates, quick clarifications, and team discussions.
- **Outlook Emails:** Best for formal announcements, detailed instructions, and important updates.
- **Face-to-Face or Virtual Meetings:** Crucial for complex or sensitive conversations, such as addressing concerns or providing feedback.

Example

During a department-wide restructuring, I used Teams for daily updates to keep the team informed about progress and next steps. Formal announcements, such as role changes or key milestones, were communicated via email with detailed instructions. For sensitive issues, like addressing redundancies, I prioritised one-to-one meetings to ensure empathy and clarity.

Ensuring Messages Are Clear, Consistent, and Timely

Inconsistent or unclear messaging creates confusion and erodes trust. A structured approach to communication can prevent misunderstandings and keep everyone aligned.

Best Practices for Clear Communication

1. **Use Plain Language:** Avoid jargon or overly complex terms, ensuring messages are accessible to all team members.
2. **Reiterate Key Points:** Repeat important messages through multiple channels to ensure they're understood.
3. **Timing Is Critical:** Deliver updates promptly, especially when addressing rumours or misinformation.

Example

During a change to clinical handover processes, I provided step-by-step guidance in an email, followed by a visual walkthrough in a team meeting. Repeating the message across formats reinforced understanding and reduced errors during implementation.

> **Reflective Questions**
> Are your messages timely, consistent, and easy to understand? How can you reinforce key points to ensure they're retained?

Involving Your Team

Engagement is a critical factor in successful change. Involving your team from the outset fosters a sense of ownership, reduces resistance, and ensures that their insights inform better outcomes.

Gathering Feedback to Increase Buy-In

Feedback provides valuable insights into how staff perceive change and what adjustments may be needed to improve its effectiveness. Inviting feedback also demonstrates respect for your team's expertise and experience.

How to Gather Feedback

- **Surveys:** Use anonymous surveys to collect honest input on how the change is progressing.
- **Focus Groups:** Facilitate small group discussions to explore concerns and generate ideas collaboratively.
- **One-to-One Check-Ins:** Create a safe space for individuals to share their thoughts privately.

Example

When introducing a new patient flow system, I held focus groups with frontline staff to identify potential barriers before implementation. Their feedback highlighted specific workflow issues we hadn't considered, allowing us to refine the system before rollout.

Recognising and Addressing Concerns Early

Resistance to change often stems from unaddressed fears or misunderstandings. Recognising and addressing concerns early helps prevent them from escalating.

Steps to Address Concerns:

1. **Listen Actively:** Pay attention to both verbal and non-verbal cues to identify underlying issues.
2. **Acknowledge Concerns:** Validate staff emotions, even if you can't fully resolve their concerns immediately.
3. **Collaborate on Solutions:** Involve staff in problem-solving to create a sense of ownership.

Example

During the introduction of new infection control protocols, several staff members expressed frustration over increased documentation requirements. By acknowledging their concerns and involving them in streamlining the process, we were able to balance compliance with efficiency.

> **Reflective Questions**
> Are you actively seeking feedback and addressing concerns? How can you create more opportunities for staff to contribute to the change process?

Supporting Individuals

Change impacts individuals differently. While some adapt quickly, others may struggle with uncertainty, stress, or resistance. As a manager, it's essential to recognise these differences and provide tailored support to ensure everyone feels valued and empowered.

Using Dynamic Conversations to Check in on Well-Being

Dynamic conversations are structured one-to-one discussions that address health, well-being, performance, and priorities. These conversations are a powerful tool for supporting individuals during change.

Best Practices for Dynamic Conversations:

1. **Create a Safe Space:** Ensure discussions are private and free from judgment.
2. **Ask Open-Ended Questions:** Encourage individuals to share their thoughts and feelings.
3. **Focus on Solutions:** Help staff identify practical steps to address their challenges.

Example

During a significant departmental restructure, I used dynamic conversations to check in with team members individually. One staff member shared concerns about balancing new responsibilities with their personal life. Together, we identified adjustments to their workload that aligned with both organisational goals and their well-being.

Recognising and Mitigating Signs of Burnout

Burnout is a common risk during periods of change, particularly in high-pressure environments like the NHS. Managers must be proactive in recognising and addressing early signs of burnout to protect staff well-being and maintain productivity.

Common Signs of Burnout

- Increased absenteeism.
- Decreased energy or enthusiasm.
- Declining performance or quality of work.

Strategies to Mitigate Burnout:

1. **Monitor Workloads:** Ensure responsibilities are distributed fairly and avoid overloading individuals.
2. **Encourage Breaks:** Promote a culture where taking breaks is seen as essential, not a weakness.
3. **Provide Support:** Offer resources such as counselling services or flexible working arrangements.

Example

During a high-stress period of implementing a new IT system, I noticed a team member becoming withdrawn and making more errors than usual. After a one-to-one discussion, we adjusted their workload and connected them with occupational health support. These steps helped them regain confidence and return to their usual performance levels.

> **Reflective Questions**
>
> Are you actively monitoring your team for signs of burnout? How can you create an environment where staff feel comfortable seeking support?

Bringing It All Together

Managing change effectively requires a combination of planning, communication, engagement, and support. By developing clear change plans with achievable goals, communicating transparently, involving your team, and supporting individuals, you can navigate transitions with confidence and compassion. These strategies not only drive successful outcomes but also reinforce trust, resilience, and alignment with NHS values.

As you apply these practical approaches, remember to reflect on your own leadership style. How can you better adapt your strategies to the unique needs of your team? Change is challenging, but with the right tools and mindset, it can also be an opportunity for growth and transformation.

Addressing Resistance and Building Resilience

Resistance to change is a natural and often unavoidable response. For NHS managers, understanding why resistance occurs and how to address it empathetically is critical to navigating transitions effectively. At the same time, fostering resilience within teams ensures they remain adaptable, motivated, and engaged, even in the face of uncertainty.

This section explores the roots of resistance, provides techniques to address it constructively, and highlights strategies for fostering resilience through a growth mindset, celebrating small successes, and maintaining morale.

Understanding Resistance

Resistance to change is not inherently negative. It often reflects a genuine concern about how change will affect individuals or the organisation. Managers who view resistance as an opportunity for dialogue, rather than an obstacle, can turn opposition into a valuable source of insight.

Why People Resist Change

Resistance is usually driven by one or more of the following factors:

1. **Fear of the Unknown**

When people don't fully understand what a change entails, they may imagine worst-case scenarios. This fear can lead to hesitation or active pushback.

Example: During the rollout of a new clinical rota system, several team members feared the change would disrupt their work-life balance. Their resistance stemmed from a lack of clarity about how the new system would work and its potential benefits.

2. **Lack of Trust**

Past experiences with poorly managed changes can erode trust in leadership. Staff may doubt whether the current change will be implemented fairly or successfully.

Example: After a failed technology implementation in one NHS Trust, staff were sceptical about subsequent IT changes, fearing another disruptive experience without tangible benefits.

3. **Perceived Loss**

Change often requires people to let go of familiar routines, tools, or roles, creating a sense of loss. This emotional response can fuel resistance.

Example: When transitioning from paper-based to electronic health records, some administrative staff resisted, feeling their expertise in managing physical records was being devalued.

Techniques to Address Resistance Empathetically

Addressing resistance requires managers to listen actively, validate concerns, and involve staff in the change process.

1. Create Open Dialogue:

Encourage staff to voice their concerns in a safe, non-judgmental environment. Use team meetings, focus groups, or one-on-one conversations to surface resistance early.

Example: In a project to redesign patient discharge processes, I hosted small workshops where staff could share their concerns and suggest improvements. This approach helped identify practical challenges and reduced resistance by involving staff in shaping the change.

2. Acknowledge and Validate Concerns:

Dismissing resistance as negativity can deepen mistrust. Instead, acknowledge the emotions behind the resistance, such as fear or frustration.

Example Dialogue: *"I understand this new system feels like a big adjustment. It's normal to feel uncertain, and I'm here to help address any concerns you have."*

3. Frame the Change Positively:

Highlight the benefits of the change, both for individuals and the organisation. Use tangible examples to show how the change aligns with NHS values like improving patient outcomes or creating a more inclusive workplace.

Example: During a department-wide restructuring, I framed the change as an opportunity to streamline workflows and create more equitable workloads, helping staff see its potential benefits.

4. Involve Staff in Problem-Solving:

Resistance often stems from a feeling of helplessness. Involving staff in finding solutions empowers them and builds ownership of the change.

Example: When implementing new infection control protocols, I invited frontline staff to co-design training materials, ensuring they were practical and relevant.

Reflective Questions

Have you created opportunities for staff to voice their concerns about change? How can you validate resistance without compromising on progress?

Fostering Resilience

Resilience is the capacity to adapt and thrive in the face of change or adversity. For NHS teams, building resilience is essential to navigating the frequent and complex changes inherent in healthcare. Managers play a crucial role in fostering this adaptability by encouraging a growth mindset, celebrating successes, and maintaining morale.

Encouraging a Growth Mindset

A growth mindset, a concept popularised by Carol Dweck, involves viewing challenges as opportunities for learning and improvement. Teams with a growth mindset are more likely to embrace change and adapt constructively.

Strategies to Foster a Growth Mindset:

1. **Model Resilience:** Demonstrate a positive attitude towards change and share examples of how you've overcome challenges in the past.
2. **Frame Challenges as Opportunities:** Emphasise how change can lead to personal or professional growth.
3. **Encourage Experimentation:** Allow staff to test new ideas and learn from mistakes without fear of judgment.

Example

In one project, we introduced a new patient triage system that required staff to learn unfamiliar software. Instead of focusing solely on the difficulties, I highlighted how mastering the system could enhance their skill sets and improve their career prospects. This reframing helped shift the team's mindset from resistance to curiosity.

> **Practical Tip**
>
> Use team meetings to celebrate examples of staff who have embraced challenges and learned new skills, reinforcing the value of a growth mindset.

Celebrating Small Successes and Maintaining Morale

Change initiatives often take time to deliver major results, which can lead to frustration or disengagement. Celebrating small wins along the way helps maintain momentum and boosts team morale.

Why Celebrating Success Matters

- **Reinforces Progress:** Highlighting achievements shows that efforts are paying off, even if the ultimate goal is still far away.
- **Boosts Confidence:** Recognising successes builds team confidence and encourages continued effort.
- **Promotes Positivity:** Celebrations create opportunities for team bonding and a sense of shared purpose.

Example

During the phased rollout of a new digital appointment booking system, we celebrated the successful training of 50 staff members by hosting a small team lunch. Recognising this milestone helped the team feel valued and motivated for the next phase.

How to Celebrate Successes

1. **Be Specific:** Identify exactly what was achieved and why it matters.
2. **Tailor Recognition:** Match the scale of the celebration to the achievement, from verbal praise in a meeting to more formal recognition.
3. **Link Successes to Goals:** Show how small wins contribute to the broader objectives of the change initiative.

Maintaining Morale During Change

Sustaining morale requires consistent effort and attention to both team dynamics and individual well-being. Managers must balance acknowledging challenges with fostering a sense of optimism and possibility.

Strategies to Maintain Morale

1. **Communicate Regularly:** Keep teams informed about progress and next steps to reduce uncertainty.
2. **Encourage Peer Support:** Create opportunities for staff to support and learn from one another, such as mentoring or buddy systems.
3. **Check in on Well-Being:** Use one-to-one conversations to address personal concerns and ensure individuals feel supported.

Example

During a challenging reorganisation, I established weekly "coffee and catch-up" sessions where team members could share updates, vent frustrations, or simply connect informally. These sessions provided a sense of normality and community amid the upheaval.

> **Reflective Questions**
>
> *How are you recognising and celebrating progress within your team? Are there ways to create more opportunities for peer support and team bonding?*

Bringing It All Together

Resistance and resilience are two sides of the same coin in change management. While resistance reflects the emotional and practical challenges people face, resilience represents their capacity to adapt and thrive. By addressing resistance empathetically and fostering resilience through a growth mindset, celebrating successes, and maintaining morale, NHS managers can create environments where change is not only managed but embraced.

As you reflect on your leadership, consider how you can better understand and address resistance within your team. Are there opportunities to validate concerns and involve staff in problem-solving? At the same time, think about how you can nurture resilience by highlighting the opportunities inherent in change, recognising progress, and building a sense of shared purpose. With these strategies, you can lead your team through uncertainty with confidence, compassion, and success.

Case Studies and Lessons Learned

Change management is as much about practical application as it is about theoretical understanding. NHS managers operate in environments where change is frequent and complex, and each situation presents unique challenges and opportunities. This section presents two real-world case studies that demonstrate how the tools and strategies outlined in this book can be effectively applied in practice.

The STAR model (Situation, Task, Actions Taken, Results) provides a structured way to illustrate the application of change management principles. These case studies highlight how the strategies and tools outlined in this book were used in real-world NHS settings, demonstrating their effectiveness in overcoming challenges and achieving positive outcomes.

Example 1: Managing a team through the NHS England merger

Situation

The NHS England merger with NHS Digital and Health Education England aimed to streamline operations and improve efficiency. While the strategic intent was clear, the merger caused significant uncertainty and anxiety at the team level. Staff were unclear about how their roles would evolve, and morale was low due to a lack of early communication about the implications of the change.

This uncertainty was compounded by fears of redundancy and concerns about how new reporting structures would impact day-to-day workflows. The team I managed expressed frustration, with some disengaging from their work and others openly voicing scepticism about the benefits of the merger.

Task

My primary task was to guide my team through this period of uncertainty, maintaining trust and productivity while aligning with organisational priorities. This required addressing morale issues, providing clarity about the transition, and involving staff in shaping the new structure to foster a sense of ownership and reduce resistance.

Actions Taken

I applied several strategies to manage the transition effectively:

1. **Clear Communication**
    - I established a regular communication cadence, including weekly email updates and Microsoft Teams meetings.
    - Updates provided clear information about what was known, acknowledged what was uncertain, and outlined timelines for decisions.

- I used team meetings to encourage open discussions, addressing rumours and reinforcing transparency.

2. **Involving the Team in Decision-Making**
   - I created working groups where staff could contribute ideas on how to adapt workflows to fit the new organisational structure.
   - These sessions ensured staff felt they had a voice in shaping the transition and reduced the feeling of being passive recipients of change.

3. **Using Dynamic Conversations to Check in on Well-Being**
   - One-to-one conversations were scheduled with each team member to understand their individual concerns and offer support.
   - These conversations were structured around the NHS **dynamic conversation pillars** (health and well-being, performance enablement, prioritisation, and aspirations).

4. **Acknowledging Emotions**
   - I explicitly validated the challenges of the "Ending, Losing, Letting Go" phase (Bridges' Transition Model).

- I acknowledged that feelings of uncertainty and frustration were natural and committed to supporting the team throughout the transition.

Results

The outcomes of these actions were clear and measurable:

1. **Improved Morale:** Regular communication and one-to-one support helped reduce anxiety, and team members reported feeling more informed and supported.
2. **Increased Engagement:** Involvement in decision-making led to a greater sense of ownership. Team members actively contributed ideas, some of which were adopted into the new workflow designs.
3. **Sustained Productivity:** Despite the challenges, the team maintained key performance metrics during the transition, with no significant drop in output.
4. **Strengthened Trust:** By prioritising transparency and empathy, trust between leadership and the team was enhanced, creating a more cohesive and resilient group.

Transparent communication, staff involvement, and individualised support are critical for managing structural change. By addressing emotional and practical concerns simultaneously, it is possible to maintain trust and productivity during transitions.

Example 2: Implementing digital systems in a Trust

Situation

An NHS Trust decided to transition from manual appointment scheduling to a digital system to reduce administrative workload and improve patient outcomes. While the new system promised long-term benefits, it was met with resistance from staff who were comfortable with the existing process. Concerns included fears about job security, doubts about the usability of the system, and apprehension about the time required for training and implementation.

Staff resistance was compounded by a lack of familiarity with similar technologies, leading to anxiety about their ability to adapt. These challenges posed a significant risk to the successful rollout of the system.

Task

My task was to ensure a smooth implementation of the digital system by:

1. Addressing staff resistance and building confidence in the new process.
2. Delivering training and support to ensure all team members could use the system effectively.

3. Demonstrating the immediate benefits of the system to build momentum and improve buy-in.

Actions Taken

I used a structured approach to address the challenges and drive the adoption of the new system:

1. **Targeted Training and Support**
   - I conducted an initial skills assessment to identify staff members who might need additional support.
   - Training sessions were designed to be interactive and hands-on, using real-life scenarios to demonstrate the system's functionality.
   - Peer mentors ("system champions") were identified to provide on-the-ground support during and after the rollout.

2. **Clear and Consistent Communication**
   - I communicated the benefits of the system through multiple channels, including emails, team briefings, and visual presentations.
   - Regular updates included feedback from pilot users to demonstrate that concerns were being addressed and the system was being refined based on staff input.

3. **Identifying Quick Wins**

- To build momentum, I focused on implementing small but impactful features first, such as automated appointment reminders.
- These quick wins demonstrated the system's potential to reduce administrative workload and improve patient satisfaction.

4. **Involving Staff in Pilot Testing**
    - A group of volunteers tested the system in a controlled environment. Their feedback was used to improve workflows before full implementation.
    - This involvement fostered ownership and reduced resistance among early adopters.

Results

The implementation was ultimately successful, with tangible benefits achieved across multiple areas:

1. **Reduced Resistance:** Targeted training and peer support significantly decreased anxiety and built confidence among staff.
2. **Increased Efficiency:** The system reduced manual workload, allowing administrative staff to focus on higher-value tasks.
3. **Improved Patient Outcomes:** Automated reminders and streamlined scheduling processes led to fewer missed appointments and better service delivery.

4. **Positive Feedback:** Staff who initially resisted the change later reported appreciating the system's efficiency and usability.

Key Lesson

Focusing on training, communication, and quick wins can transform resistance into acceptance. By involving staff early and addressing their concerns, digital transformations can be implemented with minimal disruption and maximum benefit.

Reflections on Case Studies

Both case studies demonstrate the practical application of the tools and strategies discussed in this book. From **Bridges' Transition Model** to dynamic conversations, clear communication, and quick wins, these approaches address both the technical and emotional dimensions of change.

Key Takeaways

- **Communication Is Paramount:** Whether managing structural change or introducing new technology, transparent and consistent communication reduces uncertainty and builds trust.
- **Engagement Drives Success:** Involving staff in decision-making and problem-solving fosters ownership and reduces resistance.

- **Support Is Essential:** Tailored training and individualised conversations ensure staff feel supported and empowered.
- **Celebrate Progress:** Recognising milestones, no matter how small, builds momentum and maintains morale.

By applying these strategies, NHS managers can turn the challenges of change into opportunities for growth, ensuring successful transitions that benefit both staff and patients.

Tools and Templates

Template: Change Communication Plan

A well-structured communication plan ensures that the right messages reach the right people at the right time. Use this template to outline your communication strategy for any change initiative.

1. Objectives

Define what you want to achieve through your communication efforts.

Example: Build awareness and understanding of the new system, reduce uncertainty, and ensure all staff understand their roles in the transition.

2. Stakeholder Analysis

Identify your key audiences and tailor messages accordingly.

Stakeholder Group	Concerns/Needs	Preferred Channel	Key Messages
Administrative Staff	Job security, workload impact	Email, workshops	"How this change benefits your role"
Clinical Teams	Workflow integration, patient	Meetings, Teams posts	"How this will improve efficiency"

	outcomes		
Leadership	**Progress updates, risk management**	**Reports, briefings**	**"Status and mitigation measures"**

3. Communication Channels

Choose the appropriate methods for delivering messages.

Channel	**Purpose**	**Frequency**
Microsoft Teams	Informal updates	Weekly
Email	Formal announcements	As needed
Team Meetings	Clarifications and feedback	Bi-weekly during rollout

4. Timeline

Map out your communication activities over the course of the change initiative.

Date	**Activity**	**Audience**
Week 1	Initial announcement via email	All staff
Week 2	Team meetings for Q&A sessions	Department teams
Week 3	Update on progress via Teams	All staff

5. Feedback Mechanisms

Establish ways to collect and act on feedback. Use anonymous surveys, focus groups, and one-to-one conversations to understand concerns and refine messaging.

Checklist: Key Steps for Managing Change in the NHS

This step-by-step checklist ensures you've covered all critical aspects of managing change effectively.

Planning

- Define the purpose of the change and its desired outcomes.
- Conduct a stakeholder analysis to understand who will be affected and how.
- Develop a detailed change plan with clear goals, milestones, and timelines.

Communication

- Identify key messages for different audiences and tailor them to address concerns.
- Select appropriate communication channels (e.g., Teams for informal updates, Outlook for formal announcements).
- Create a timeline for communication activities to ensure consistency.

Engagement

- Involve staff in the planning process to foster ownership and reduce resistance.
- Gather feedback through surveys, focus groups, or one-to-one conversations.
- Acknowledge and address concerns early in the process.

Implementation

- Pilot new processes or systems to test feasibility and address issues before full rollout.
- Provide targeted training to ensure staff feel confident in their new roles or tools.
- Identify and celebrate quick wins to build momentum and morale.

Support

- Check in regularly with team members to monitor their well-being and address burnout.
- Use dynamic conversations to explore individual challenges and provide tailored support.
- Foster resilience by encouraging a growth mindset and recognising progress.

Evaluation

- Measure progress against defined milestones and adjust plans as needed.

- Collect feedback on the effectiveness of the change process and identify lessons learned.
- Share successes and reflections with the team to reinforce trust and learning.

Tool: Resilience-Building Activities for Teams

Building resilience within teams is essential to navigating the ongoing changes in the NHS. These activities are designed to foster adaptability, teamwork, and a positive mindset.

Activity 1: Growth Mindset Reflections

Purpose: Encourage individuals to view challenges as opportunities for learning.

How to Use:
1. In a team meeting, ask each person to share an example of a recent challenge they overcame and what they learned.
2. Discuss as a group how these lessons can be applied to current or future changes.
3. Reinforce the idea that setbacks are part of growth.

Activity 2: Celebrating Small Wins

Purpose: Boost morale by recognising progress and contributions.

How to Use:

1. At the end of each week, hold a brief team huddle to highlight achievements, no matter how small.
2. Invite team members to nominate colleagues who have made positive contributions during the week.
3. Use simple rewards like verbal praise, certificates, or small treats to acknowledge efforts.

Activity 3: Resilience Mapping

Purpose: Help teams identify their strengths and areas for improvement in responding to change.

How to Use:
1. Provide each team member with a worksheet divided into three sections:
    - **What we do well:** List strengths in handling change (e.g., collaboration, adaptability).
    - **What we can improve:** Identify challenges or gaps (e.g., communication, time management).
    - **What support we need:** Specify resources or actions that would help (e.g., training, feedback).
2. Discuss the results as a team and create an action plan to address identified needs.

Bringing It All Together

These tools and templates are designed to help you implement the strategies outlined in this book effectively. Whether you're planning a change initiative, communicating with stakeholders, or supporting your team's resilience, these resources provide a practical starting point. By tailoring them to your specific context, you can lead with confidence and achieve meaningful outcomes that benefit both your team and the patients they serve.

Reflection and Next Steps

Change is a constant in the NHS, but how we approach and manage it determines its success. Throughout this guide, we've explored the complexities of change management, practical strategies, and tools to support both your team and yourself. Now, it's time to take these insights and translate them into action.

This section encourages you to reflect on your experiences with change, outlines actionable steps to implement the lessons from this guide, and highlights resources for ongoing support and professional development.

Encouraging Reflection

Self-reflection is an essential skill for managers navigating change. It allows you to evaluate past experiences, identify areas for growth, and build on your strengths. Taking time to reflect not only enhances your personal development but also equips you to lead with greater confidence and clarity.

Questions for Reflection

1. **What Have You Learned from Past Change Initiatives?**
    - Think about the successes and challenges of past changes.

- What worked well? What could you have done differently?

2. **How Do You Typically Respond to Resistance?**
   - Reflect on how you've handled resistance within your team.
   - Were you able to identify and address the underlying concerns?

3. **How Resilient Is Your Team?**
   - Consider how your team copes with uncertainty and setbacks.
   - What strategies can you adopt to strengthen their resilience?

Example Reflection:

During a reorganisation, I realised that my initial focus on logistics overshadowed the emotional impact on my team. Reflecting on this, I've committed to prioritising psychological safety and open dialogue in future changes.

Actionable Steps to Implement Lessons

While theory provides the foundation, actionable steps ensure real-world impact. Here's how you can apply the lessons from this guide:

1. Develop a Change Plan
   - **Set Goals and Milestones:** Clearly define what success looks like and break the change into manageable phases.
   - **Identify Quick Wins:** Focus on small, achievable goals to build early momentum.

Action Example: Begin your next change initiative by mapping out a communication plan using the provided template to ensure clarity and consistency.

2. Enhance Communication Practices
   - Use multiple channels to ensure everyone receives the information they need.
   - Regularly check for understanding and address feedback promptly.

Action Example: Schedule weekly Microsoft Teams updates for informal progress sharing, supplemented by formal email summaries.

3. Foster Team Involvement
   - Create opportunities for staff to contribute ideas and voice concerns.
   - Actively involve team members in pilot testing or decision-making processes.

Action Example: Host a workshop where staff can co-design workflows for a new process, increasing their sense of ownership.

4. Build Psychological Safety

- Encourage open conversations about challenges and uncertainties.
- Use one-to-one dynamic conversations to check in on individual well-being.

Action Example: During a team meeting, share a personal example of overcoming change-related challenges to model vulnerability and build trust.

5. Celebrate Successes

- Recognise and reward achievements, no matter how small.
- Link celebrations to organisational values to reinforce their importance.

Action Example: After successfully completing the first phase of a rollout, host a team lunch to thank staff for their contributions.

Where to Go for Additional Support

Managing change can feel isolating, but a wealth of resources is available to support you in this journey. From NHS-specific tools to external training opportunities, these resources can help you refine your skills and stay informed about best practices.

NHS Resources

NHS Leadership Academy
Offers training programs, workshops, and resources focused on leadership and change management.

People Promise Resources
Tools and guides aligned with the NHS People Promise to promote inclusion, collaboration, and psychological safety.

Dynamic Conversations Framework
Use this NHS-specific approach for structured one-to-one discussions with team members.

External Training Opportunities

Chartered Management Institute (CMI)

Offers accredited courses in change management, leadership, and resilience.

British Psychological Society (BPS)

Provides resources on workplace psychology, including managing resistance and fostering resilience.

Online Learning Platforms

Platforms like Coursera and LinkedIn Learning offer flexible courses on change management and leadership.

Peer Networks and Communities

NHS Networks

Join forums or professional groups to share experiences and learn from colleagues.

Mentorship Programs

Seek guidance from experienced leaders within your organisation or professional community.

Final Thoughts

Change is never easy, but with the right tools, mindset, and support, it can be a transformative experience for both you and your team. This guide has provided a roadmap for navigating change, grounded in practical strategies and real-world examples. As you move forward, remember:

Reflect on Your Practice: Take time to evaluate your experiences and learn from them.

Empower Your Team: Involve them in the journey, listen to their concerns, and celebrate their contributions.

Invest in Your Development: Continuously seek opportunities to enhance your skills and knowledge.

By embracing these principles, you can lead with confidence, resilience, and compassion, ensuring that change becomes an opportunity for growth rather than a source of fear. The NHS will always face challenges, but with capable, reflective managers at the helm, those challenges can be met with innovation, collaboration, and success.

Now, it's your turn. Take the insights from this guide and put them into action, shaping the future of healthcare leadership, one step at a time.

Conclusion

Change in the NHS is both inevitable and essential. It drives progress, improves patient outcomes, and ensures the organisation can adapt to ever-evolving challenges. Yet, the human impact of change is profound, and how it is managed can make the difference between success and failure. As a manager, you are not just an implementer of change; you are a guide, a communicator, and a source of stability for your team.

The Importance of Proactive, Compassionate Leadership

At the heart of effective change management is leadership that is both proactive and compassionate. By anticipating challenges, engaging with your team, and addressing concerns empathetically, you create an environment where people feel supported and valued, even during uncertainty.

Compassionate leadership isn't a soft skill—it's a critical strategy. It builds trust, fosters collaboration, and ensures your team feels empowered to embrace change rather than resist it. Proactivity complements compassion, enabling you to set clear goals, communicate effectively, and make decisions with confidence. Together, these qualities form the foundation for leading change successfully.

Key Takeaways

Proactive Leadership: Be clear about the vision for change, anticipate challenges, and prepare your team to adapt.

Compassionate Leadership: Acknowledge the emotional impact of change, validate concerns, and offer support throughout the transition.

Empowering Managers to Lead Confidently

Leadership during change is challenging, but it is also an opportunity to inspire growth and resilience in your team. The tools and strategies in this guide are designed to help you navigate the complexities of change with confidence. Whether you are managing structural reorganisations, embedding cultural shifts, or implementing new technologies, the principles of transparency, involvement, and support remain constant.

As you lead, remember these key principles:
Communicate with Clarity and Consistency: Ensure your team understands the "why," "what," and "how" of change.

Involve Your Team: Encourage collaboration and input to foster ownership and reduce resistance.

Support Individuals: Recognise that each team member experiences change differently, and provide personalised support where needed.

Celebrate Progress: Acknowledge small successes to build momentum and reinforce morale.

Your role as a leader extends beyond managing tasks—it's about inspiring your team to see change as an opportunity for growth rather than a threat. By leading with confidence and compassion, you can create an environment where your team thrives, even in the face of uncertainty.

Looking Ahead

The NHS will continue to evolve, and with it, the challenges of leading in an ever-changing environment. As a manager, your ability to adapt, reflect, and lead proactively will be critical to your success and the success of your team. This guide has provided you with a framework to navigate change effectively, but the journey doesn't end here. Learning, growth, and resilience are ongoing processes, and every change initiative presents a new opportunity to develop as a leader.

As you reflect on the insights and strategies shared in this guide, take pride in the vital role you play in shaping the future of healthcare. Your leadership has the power to transform uncertainty into opportunity, resistance into collaboration, and challenges into successes. The NHS needs confident, compassionate managers like you to lead the way.

Go forward with the tools, strategies, and confidence to make a meaningful impact—not just for your team, but for the patients and communities you serve.

About the author

Matthew Miles is an experienced leader in healthcare management, specialising in organisational development, data-driven decision-making, and team leadership within the NHS. With over a decade of experience, Matt has worked in national NHS central functions and large NHS Trusts, successfully managing teams, navigating complex system changes, and driving improvements in patient outcomes and operational efficiency.

Matt has held senior management roles overseeing large multidisciplinary teams delivering critical functions such as data registration and management, operational and analytical roles, and strategic project delivery. His work has directly contributed to enhancing healthcare services, informing national policies, and supporting research that improves patient care. From overseeing high-stakes data management projects to implementing innovative digital systems, Matt has consistently demonstrated his ability to lead through challenge and change.

As a Chartered Manager and Fellow of the Chartered Management Institute (CMI), Matt is recognised for his expertise in leadership and strategic management. He is also a Chartered IT Professional with the British Computer Society (BCS), which reflects his ability to align technology with healthcare operations effectively. These professional credentials underscore his commitment to excellence and continuous learning in a rapidly evolving sector.

Key highlights of Matt's career include:
- Leading teams through complex organisational restructures within NHS settings, maintaining morale and performance during periods of uncertainty.
- Successfully transitioning manual systems to digital workflows, reducing errors, improving efficiency, and enhancing patient care.
- Developing strategies to foster inclusive, collaborative team cultures, aligned with NHS values of compassion, respect, and excellence.

Matt's approach to leadership combines empathy with pragmatism. He is deeply passionate about creating environments where individuals and teams feel supported, empowered, and motivated to achieve their best. His leadership style is rooted in psychological safety, continuous improvement, and a commitment to bringing out the potential in others.

Beyond his professional achievements, Matt is a strong advocate for balancing professional and personal life. He is a devoted stepdad to three children and partner to husband, Steve. A keen photographer and scuba diver, Matt enjoys exploring creativity and adventure in his personal time. He also has a passion for technology, applying innovative solutions to enhance everyday living.

With his extensive experience in healthcare management and leadership, Matt is uniquely positioned to offer practical insights and tools for NHS managers. His writing reflects a deep understanding of the challenges leaders face, providing actionable advice to help them thrive in one of the most demanding yet rewarding sectors.

Call to action

Thank you for reading **Managing Through Change**. If you found this book valuable, I would greatly appreciate it if you could take a moment to leave a review on Amazon. Your feedback helps others discover this resource and supports the creation of more practical guides for NHS leaders.